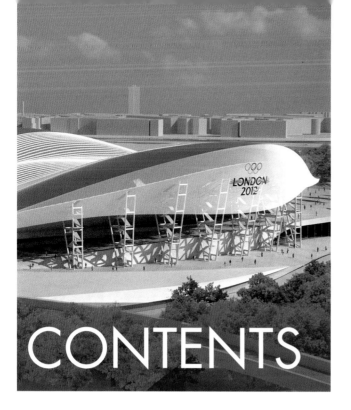

CONTENTS

Image courtesy of London 2012; an artist's impression of the Aquatics Centre during the Games

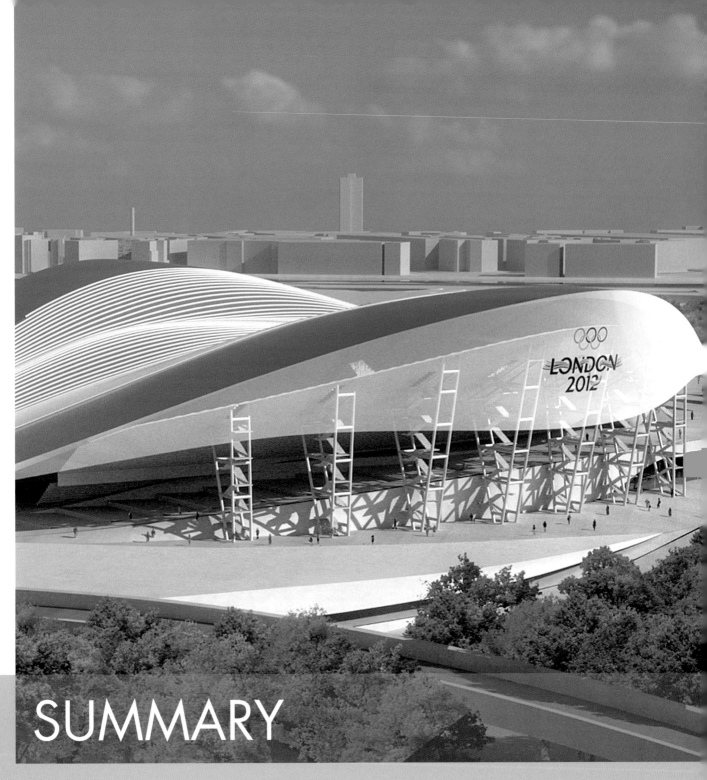

SUMMARY

1   This is the first in a series of National Audit Office reports on the preparations for hosting the London 2012 Olympic and Paralympic Games. It is an early look at the progress that has been made to put in place the necessary delivery and financial arrangements since London was chosen as the host city on 6 July 2005. In most areas the arrangements are still being developed or are bedding down, and the report therefore identifies key risks and challenges going forward.

2   In future reports we will examine how the delivery and financial arrangements are working in practice and track progress in preparing for the Games. In addition, we will be reviewing the work to establish the budget for the Olympic programme, with a view to reporting our findings when the budget has been finalised.

National Audit Office

WITHDRAWN
FROM STOCK
QMUL LIBRARY

ndon 2012
c Games –
anagement

LONDON: The Stationery Office
£13.50

Ordered by the
House of Commons
to be printed on 30 January 2007

REPORT BY THE COMPTROLLER AND AUDITOR GENERAL | HC 252 Session 2006-2007 | 2 February 2007

This report has been prepared under Section 6
of the National Audit Act 1983 for presentation
to the House of Commons in accordance with
Section 9 of the Act.

John Bourn
Comptroller and Auditor General
National Audit Office

29 January 2007

The National Audit Office
study team consisted of:

Laura Brackwell, Mark Garrety, Keith Hawkswell
and Gareth Tuck. Ailbhe McNabola and
Lesley Whitworth assisted with parts of the study.

This report can be found on the National Audit
Office web site at www.nao.org.uk

For further information about the
National Audit Office please contact:

National Audit Office
Press Office
157-197 Buckingham Palace Road
Victoria
London
SW1W 9SP

Tel: 020 7798 7400

Email: enquiries@nao.gsi.gov.uk

© National Audit Office 2007

3   Our main findings are as follows.

■   Progress has been made in putting in place the key delivery structures, including setting up the Olympic Delivery Authority, the London Organising Committee of the Olympic Games and Paralympic Games (LOCOG), and the Olympic Lottery Distributor, and work is ongoing to develop underpinning practices and procedures. The delivery structures are complex, however, and this does bring the risk of cumbersome decision making.

■   The layout of the Olympic Park has been finalised, nearly all the land has been acquired, and work on the physical site is underway. The Olympic Delivery Authority has published a draft Transport Plan for consultation and is preparing the Olympic planning applications. Work is also ongoing to finalise proposals for the legacy use and ownership of the venues, and to develop plans for delivering and measuring the wider benefits of the Games, a key driver behind London's bid.

■   There has been a good deal of work on the cost estimates for the Olympic venues, associated infrastructure and other non-staging costs. In November 2006 the Secretary of State for Culture, Media and Sport reported that, although some offsetting savings have been identified, overall the cost estimates for the the Olympic Park have increased by some £900 million. A number of areas of uncertainty remain and there continues to be no final agreed budget, with implications for budgetary planning and control. Substantial further public funding is likely to be required in addition to the public sector funding package of £2.375 billion that was agreed before the bid. The Government is also to provide £1.044 billion towards the costs of infrastructure on the site of the Olympic Park. LOCOG has a budget of £2 billion for staging the Games. As required by the International Olympic Committee, the Government has underwritten the costs of the Games.

■   Across the Olympic programme as a whole, the Olympic Programme Support Unit has been set up to track progress and key risks, and provide the Olympic Board with the information it needs to make decisions. Within central government, the Government Olympic Executive will play a key role in co-ordinating the various contributions that government departments will make to the Games and in overseeing the Olympic Delivery Authority, LOCOG and the Olympic Lottery Distributor.

4   Our overall conclusion is that the key relationships and working arrangements to deliver the Olympic programme are still being developed. There are a number of areas of risk that will need to be managed but a major risk is the lack of final agreed cost estimates and an accompanying funding package, and this will inevitably have a detrimental impact on the programme if it is allowed to continue.

Recommendations

5   The main areas of risk that need to be managed for the successful delivery of the Games are set out in **Figure 1**. The risks are, of course, interdependent – failure in any one area will impinge on others. At the end of each section of the report are boxes setting out what we see as the key actions required to manage the risks. These points do not imply a lack of attention on the part of those involved; indeed much has been done and is being done. Nevertheless, with 18 months of the timetable of 84 months now elapsed, it is essential to keep the momentum up so that progress is maintained.

---

1   Main areas of risk that need to be managed for successful delivery of the Games

1   Delivering the Games against an immovable deadline.

2   The need for strong governance and delivery structures given the multiplicity of organisations and groups involved in the Games.

3   The requirement for the budget to be clearly determined and effectively managed.

4   Applying effective procurement practices.

5   Planning for a lasting legacy.

6   The installation of effective progress monitoring and risk management arrangements.

Source: National Audit Office

---

6 Within the key actions required to manage risk, we have identified four aspects which require particular attention now.

a **Finalising the cost estimates and funding package.** Establishing a robust lifetime budget for the venues and infrastructure for the Games would allow the programme to move forward with greater confidence and certainty, and with a better basis for financial control. There are clearly some difficult decisions and judgements to be made in finalising the budget but the Department for Culture, Media and Sport needs to work with the Treasury, the Greater London Authority, and other parties as necessary, to resolve this as a matter of urgency.

b **Delivering clear and quick decision making on individual projects and at programme level.** Reflecting in part the multiple stakeholders and sources of funding, and the requirements of the International Olympic Committee, responsibility for decision making rests not with any one individual but with all those organisations involved in delivering and funding the Games. In any programme where there are multiple stakeholders, a pre-requisite for achieving smooth decision making is establishing a common understanding of how the motivations and actions of individual bodies impact on the programme as a whole so that possible areas of tension can be identified early.

c **Maintaining an effective Olympic Programme Support Unit.** Although only a small team, the Unit has a pivotal role to play in supporting the Olympic Board in its oversight of the programme. To be in a position to provide independent and authoritative advice, the Unit needs to have the necessary skills and authority to probe and engage actively with the individual stakeholders, who in turn must support the Unit by sharing information and being open to challenge.

d **Achieving effective government oversight.** To be in a position to exercise effective oversight of the Olympic Delivery Authority and LOCOG, the Government Olympic Executive needs the necessary authority and technical expertise to monitor and challenge on an equal footing. As we were finalising this report, and following a review initiated by the new Permanent Secretary in November 2006, the Department announced it would be appointing a new Director General and Financial Director for the Government Olympic Executive with high-level commercial and financial experience and expertise in major, complex infrastructure programmes. The Permanent Secretary also announced that he would be taking on the Accounting Officer function for the Games which has previously sat with the Chief Executive of the Government Olympic Executive. A key question for the Government Olympic Executive will be judging how 'hands on' it is appropriate to be at any particular time and getting the right balance between allowing the experts in these organisations to get on and deliver and providing the degree of challenge which is a key part of good governance and accountability for public money.

MAIN REPORT

7   This report is our first about the preparations for the London 2012 Olympic and Paralympic Games. Background facts about the Games are set out in Appendix 1.

8   Delivering and funding the Olympic programme involves many bodies, but the primary focus of our work was the Department for Culture, Media and Sport (the Department), the lead government department for the Games, and the Olympic Delivery Authority, which is taking forward over the next few years the work to deliver the Olympic venues and infrastructure.

9   The methods we used are described in Appendix 2. Our work was informed by the experience of other host cities, including Sydney (2000), Athens (2004), Beijing (2008) and Vancouver (which will host the Winter Games in 2010). We reviewed audit reports on these Games, and have arranged with the Auditor General in China to learn lessons from 2008 that could be usefully applied to London.

10   We have organised the report around six over-arching risks which will need to be managed throughout the years leading up to 2012. A box at the end of each section sets out key actions required to manage the risk area in question.

Risk area 1: Delivering the Games against an immovable deadline

11   The Olympics will begin in London on 27 July 2012 and end on 12 August, with the Paralympics following from 29 August to 9 September 2012, so the organisations involved in delivering the Games have a fixed deadline.

12   The Olympic programme comprises a series of individual but interdependent projects. Effective project management works on the basis of a 'time/cost/quality triangle' where changes in one factor may mean trade-offs in one or both of the other factors. So the set deadline for the Games means any delay to elements of the delivery programme risks putting pressure on cost and/or quality. Delay may weaken negotiating positions on contracts, additional resources may have to be brought in to bring projects back on schedule, or the specification of venues may have to be changed to allow them to be completed on time or to contain costs.

13   In broad terms, the delivery programme set out by the Olympic Delivery Authority for the seven years from London being awarded the Games in July 2005 is: two years to acquire and prepare the land, secure planning permissions, and do the design work and procurement; four years to build the venues and infrastructure; and one year to fit out the venues for the Games and stage test events.

14   Other sections of this report cover the progress that has been made in areas such as setting up new organisations and letting contracts, but in terms of delivering the physical site, progress has been concentrated in three main areas – the project to re-route power lines underground, assembling the land required, and finalising the design of the Olympic Park.

Re-routing the power lines underground

15   The overhead power lines on the area of the Olympic Park are to be re-routed through new cables in two six kilometre long tunnels, some 30 metres below ground. To make early progress the contract for this project was let by the London Development Agency prior to the establishment of the Olympic Delivery Authority, and the Department secured Exchequer funding for the work, paying out £36 million in 2005-06. In total, the project is expected to cost £231.6 million and the contract transferred to the Authority in November 2006. Prior to the transfer, the Authority commissioned a report by its internal auditors which underlined the criticality of the project and made recommendations designed to strengthen project management and governance.

16   Tunnelling work has begun and is generally on schedule for completion in 2007 to be followed by cable laying and commissioning. During Summer 2008 power is planned to be switched from overground to underground, allowing removal of the overhead cables and electricity pylons, freeing up the Olympic Park site for development.

Assembling the land

17   The Olympic Park site covers some 500 acres of previously used and contaminated land in the Lower Lea Valley in East London, an area equivalent in size to Hyde Park. Acquiring the land is the responsibility of the London Development Agency, which has a budget of £665 million for this, money that is additional to the public funding that has been agreed for the Games (paragraph 44).

18   By July 2006 the London Development Agency had assembled more than 90 per cent of the land through agreements with land owners and occupiers. The public inquiry on the Compulsory Purchase Order[1] to acquire the remaining land has been completed and in December 2006 the Order was confirmed by the Secretary of State for Trade and Industry. The Agency aims to have possession of the whole site by Summer 2007 and will retain ownership of the land throughout the Olympic programme and beyond.

19   In May 2006 the London Development Agency also appointed the two main contractors who will carry out remediation and demolition work to prepare the site so that construction can begin. The contracts are to transfer to the Olympic Delivery Authority, and will be co-funded by the Authority and the London Development Agency.

Finalising the design of the Olympic Park

20   Work has been ongoing to finalise the plans for the design and layout of the Olympic Park (the 'masterplan') which were outlined in London's bid to host the Games. Finalising the masterplan is a key milestone, reducing the risks of delay and increased cost which come with change at a later stage.

21   In January 2006 the interim Olympic Delivery Authority announced changes to the plans in the bid to optimise the layout of the venues and facilities and enhance legacy benefits. The changes also reduced the amount of land required for the Games, meaning that fewer businesses needed to relocate. An amended masterplan was announced in June 2006 reflecting the changes, and the Authority is currently working up environmental and transport impact assessments to support the submission of planning applications in January 2007. In October 2006 the Authority also published a draft Transport Plan for the Games for consultation, a process which will run until February 2007.

---

1   The Compulsory Purchase Order process includes a public inquiry where an independent inspector considers the Order and hears objections. In the light of the evidence, the inspector makes a recommendation to the Secretary of State for Trade and Industry, who then decides whether to confirm the Order.

22   All the changes to the design of the Olympic Park have been approved by the International Olympic Committee. Appendix 3 shows the location of the Olympic venues and the design of the Olympic Park.

Overall progress

23   The stakeholders we interviewed were generally of the view that good progress had been made since London was awarded the Games, although they stressed the tightness of the timetable that lay ahead. And in November 2006 the Chairman of the International Olympic Committee's Co-ordination Commission[2] reported that he was happy with the progress taking place in London.

24   The Olympic Delivery Authority's focus is now moving from 'start up' to being fully operational, and it is taking forward work to finalise the scope, budget and timetable of individual projects and schedule them into an overall programme. The Authority's spending is behind what was projected, totalling £75.3 million in the first six months of 2006-07 compared with profiled expenditure of £90.6 million. The underspend reflects a rescheduling of work on environmental and transport impact assessments until after the review of the Olympic Park masterplan (see paragraph 21) and slower than anticipated staff recruitment.

RISK AREA 1

Delivering the Games against an immovable deadline – action required to manage risk

■ Making sure the timetable for constructing and testing the venues and infrastructure is adhered to, thereby avoiding the pressures on cost and quality that could come from delays giving rise to:

  ■ a weakened negotiating position;

  ■ increased levels of inflation in the construction industry resulting from unplanned surges in demand; and

  ■ having to compromise on design and long term legacy value.

The other sections of this report identify steps designed to help ensure that the Olympic programme progresses on schedule.

Risk area 2: The need for strong governance and delivery structures given the multiplicity of organisations and groups involved in the Games

25   There are three principal stakeholders in the delivery of the 2012 Games – the Government (represented by the Department for Culture, Media and Sport – the Secretary of State is the Olympics Minister, with Olympic matters overseen by a Cabinet Committee[3]), the Mayor of London and the British Olympic Association. In addition to these three, a series of other bodies are involved to a greater or lesser extent in delivering or funding the Games. A summary of the structures is shown in **Figure 2 overleaf**, with more detail of the organisations and groups involved set out in Appendix 4.

26   The commitments made in London's bid for the Games and the requirements of the Host City Contract with the International Olympic Committee have been translated into a vision – "to host an inspirational, safe and inclusive Olympic and Paralympic Games and leave a sustainable legacy for London and the UK". The vision is supported by a series of objectives and sub-objectives, each of which has been assigned to a lead stakeholder to develop delivery plans (Appendix 5).

The Olympic Delivery Authority and LOCOG

27   Most of the organisations shown in Figure 2 already existed in July 2005 when London was chosen to host the Games but two new bodies have been set up to take the lead in delivering the Games – the Olympic Delivery Authority and the London Organising Committee of the Olympic Games and Paralympic Games (LOCOG) **(Figure 3 on page 11)**. The International Olympic Committee requires host cities to establish an Organising Committee to stage the Games, and the Department decided to set up a separate Olympic Delivery Authority in view of the different skills needed first to deliver the venues and infrastructure and then to stage the Games. Recognising the different skills needed at different phases of major projects was highlighted in the Comptroller and Auditor General's report[4] as one of the key lessons to emerge from the experience of the Millennium Dome, but it will be important for the two organisations to work effectively together for the benefit of the programme as a whole.

---

2   The Co-ordination Commission is formed shortly after the election of a host city to oversee and assist the Organising Committee in the planning, construction, and implementation of the Games.

3   The Ministerial Committee on Olympic and Paralympic Games (MISC 25) whose role is to co-ordinate and oversee Government issues relating to the London 2012 Olympic and Paralympic Games.

4   *The Millennium Dome* (HC 936, Session 1999-2000).

2   Summary of the delivery structures for the 2012 Games

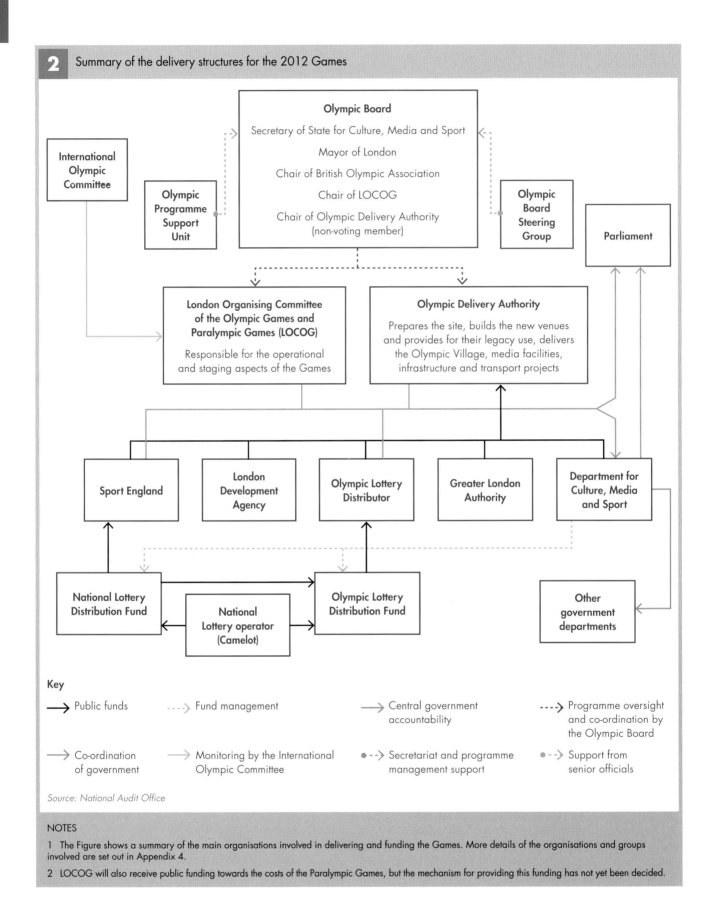

Key

→ Public funds

╌╌→ Fund management

→ Central government accountability

╌╌→ Programme oversight and co-ordination by the Olympic Board

→ Co-ordination of government

→ Monitoring by the International Olympic Committee

●╌→ Secretariat and programme management support

●╌→ Support from senior officials

Source: National Audit Office

NOTES

1   The Figure shows a summary of the main organisations involved in delivering and funding the Games. More details of the organisations and groups involved are set out in Appendix 4.

2   LOCOG will also receive public funding towards the costs of the Paralympic Games, but the mechanism for providing this funding has not yet been decided.

3   The new delivery organisations for the 2012 Games

The Olympic Delivery Authority

- Will prepare the Olympic Park site, build the new venues and provide for their legacy use, and deliver the Olympic Village, media facilities, infrastructure and transport projects for the Games.

- A non-departmental public body, overseen by the Department for Culture, Media and Sport, established by the London Olympic Games and Paralympic Games Act 2006.

The London Organising Committee of the Olympic Games and Paralympic Games (LOCOG)

- Responsible for the operational and staging aspects of the Games.

- A company limited by guarantee, and a body within the central government sector, established by a joint venture agreement between the Secretary of State for Culture, Media and Sport, the Mayor of London and the British Olympic Association. Within central government LOCOG is overseen by the Department for Culture, Media and Sport.

- The liaison point for the International Olympic Committee and a party to the Host City Contract with the International Olympic Committee, which was signed by the Mayor of London on behalf of the city and the British Olympic Association.

Source: National Audit Office

28   The bids for the 2012 Games were the first where candidate cities were required to submit an integrated bid to host the Olympic and Paralympic Games, and LOCOG is therefore responsible for organising both events. The British Paralympic Association is represented on LOCOG's Board and the Olympic Board Steering Group, and the Association stressed to us the importance of the Paralympics being embedded into the mainstream delivery structures and planning.

29   Getting the new organisations up and running once London had been awarded the Games was a priority.

- Initially to get things moving an interim Olympic Delivery Authority was operated by the London Development Agency and Transport for London. The Chief Executive was appointed in January 2006 and he was supported by a small executive team of interim appointments. The Olympic Delivery Authority itself came into being on 1 April 2006 once the necessary legislation had been passed. The Authority took slightly longer than planned to get its executive management team in place but by September 2006 other directors had taken up post, and some 50 staff had been recruited out of an expected final total of around 200. The Authority's operating costs for 2006-07 are expected to be around £25 million. The Authority is expected to be wound up by 2014 after the venues have been converted for their legacy use.

- LOCOG has evolved from the London 2012 bid team and has also made a number of new senior appointments, including the Chief Executive. At September 2006 it had 100 staff but will expand to some 3,000 as the Games draw closer. LOCOG's operating costs for 2006-07 are expected to be £26 million. LOCOG is due to be wound up at around the end of 2012.

The new lottery distribution arrangements

30   The Department has also introduced new distribution arrangements – the Olympic Lottery Distribution Fund and the Olympic Lottery Distributor – to handle the lottery funding that will be raised for the Games. Rather than extending the role of an existing lottery distributor, the Department opted to set up a new distributor in order to have a small organisation focused exclusively on the Games. The Olympic Lottery Distributor is expected to have up to 10 staff and operating costs of up to £480,000 in 2006-07.

The Olympic Board

31 The Olympic programme is overseen by the Olympic Board, which was established by a memorandum of understanding between the Secretary of State for Culture, Media and Sport, the Mayor of London and the British Olympic Association. The memorandum sets out the Board's responsibilities as "to resolve and determine issues raised by members of the Board to ensure the delivery of the Games; and to ensure that a sustainable legacy is achieved following the staging of the Games".

32 The Olympic Board comprises the Secretary of State for Culture, Media and Sport, the Mayor of London, and the Chairs of the British Olympic Association and LOCOG. Given the Olympic Delivery Authority's central role in delivering the Games, its Chair also attends Board meetings as a non-voting member. To support the Board there is a Steering Group of senior officials (including the Chief Executives of the Government Olympic Executive, the Olympic Delivery Authority and LOCOG) and an Olympic Programme Support Unit, which has a secretariat and programme management function.

33 The Olympic Board is chaired alternately by the Secretary of State and the Mayor of London. It aims to take decisions by unanimous consensus, although matters can be decided by majority vote if needed. No member of the Board has a casting vote but each has individual 'consent rights', a potential veto, over certain key decisions which affect their particular responsibilities.

Co-ordination of the Government's interest

34 To manage the Government's interest in the Games and provide cross-government co-ordination, a new dedicated team, the Government Olympic Executive, has been set up within the Department for Culture, Media and Sport. The Executive is building its capacity and will have some 35 staff, with running costs of some £3 million a year. It is led by a Chief Executive, who was designated as the Accounting Officer for the Games by the departmental Accounting Officer, who retained over-arching responsibility for all the Department's activities.

35 Given the contribution other parts of government will make to the successful delivery of the Games, the role of the Government Olympic Executive is crucial. Its Chief Executive chairs an Inter-Departmental Steering Group whose role is to co-ordinate at a strategic level the Government's interests and responsibilities. Below this group is an Olympic Co-ordinators Group, comprising those with day-to-day responsibility for Olympic issues. The Executive also oversees the Olympic Delivery Authority, LOCOG and the Olympic Lottery Distributor.

Decision making arrangements

36 The delivery structures for the Games are complex, reflecting in part the multiple stakeholders and sources of funding, and the requirements of the International Olympic Committee (see paragraph 27). The structures mean that there are numerous interfaces between organisations and a framework of legal and financial documents has been put in place to manage these relationships. Practical working arrangements and protocols are now being developed and supporting working groups established, such as the Olympic Funders Forum (see paragraph 52).

37 Nevertheless the complexity of the delivery structures, combined with the fact that no one individual has overall responsibility for delivering the Games, does bring the risk of cumbersome decision making. So a key challenge going forward will be for the structures to provide clear and quick decision making so the delivery programme is not held up. Effective decision making is especially important for projects on the critical path, such as the construction of the main Olympic stadium where decisions about legacy use are being revisited and the Olympic Delivery Authority's procurement process is ongoing alongside the continuing discussions about legacy.

38 To facilitate decision making, the Department has established an Olympic Projects Review Group, chaired by the Government Olympic Executive, to assess whether significant projects[5] can be recommended to the Secretary of State for Culture, Media and Sport, the Treasury and the Mayor of London for financial approval. The Review Group aims to make recommendations within two weeks.

---

5   The Olympic Projects Review Group will consider projects which are above the Olympic Delivery Authority's financial delegation limit of £20 million or which are deemed "novel or contentious".

RISK AREA 2

The need for strong governance and delivery structures given the multiplicity of organisations and groups involved in the Games – action required to manage risk

a   Maintaining a clear focus on the need for timely decision making individually and collectively on a programme where there are multiple stakeholders and interests.

b   Monitoring the performance of the Olympic Projects Review Group in facilitating timely decision making on significant projects.

c   Co-ordinating the multiple contributions to the Games. Within central government, the Government Olympic Executive's leadership role will be crucial and the Executive will need the authority and technical skills to challenge and influence effectively, and to oversee an administratively and logistically complex programme of this kind.

d   Developing human resources strategies for the duration of the programme given the challenges of recruiting and retaining the right people for what is by definition time limited employment, and of changing skills needs as the programme progresses.

e   Ensuring that the arrangements for planning and delivering the Games reflect throughout the aim of these being fully integrated Olympic and Paralympic Games.

Risk area 3: The requirement for the budget to be clearly determined and effectively managed

39   This section considers the budget for the Games, specifically: the cost estimates at the time of the bid; the public funding for the Games agreed prior to the bid being made; developments since London was chosen to host the Games; LOCOG's budget for staging the Games; the importance of being clear about the cost of the Games; and the need for strong financial management and control.

40   As required by the International Olympic Committee, the Government is the ultimate guarantor of funding for the Games, underwriting the costs of the infrastructure, venues and facilities, and any shortfall between LOCOG's costs and revenues. The Government's commitment to act as the guarantor was notified to Parliament as a contingent liability in December 2003 before the bid was made.

The cost estimates at the time of the bid

41   The Department started to develop cost estimates for the Games in 2002 before the decision to bid was made. The estimates at the time of the bid were based on a review by PricewaterhouseCoopers, who were commissioned to identify the costs and revenues related both to the Games and to the regeneration of the Lower Lea Valley in East London.

42   **Figure 4 overleaf** shows the costs that were expected at the time of the bid to be covered by the public sector funding package for the Games (**see Figure 5 on page 15**). The International Olympic Committee had set out its information requirements in the instructions to Candidate Cities, and this prescribed the information that was required to be submitted in the Candidate File in November 2004. The cost estimates in the Candidate File were expressed in US dollars at 2004 prices. Figure 4 also sets out the equivalent cash outturn estimates at the time of the bid, taking into account assumptions about price inflation.

43   The Candidate File described capital investment for venues and facilities, Olympic Park infrastructure, and roads and railways, which was to be financed by a combination of the public sector funding package to the extent that the work was Olympic related (for Olympic related costs see paragraph 70), and further contributions from the public and private sectors. The costs were estimated in pounds sterling and converted into US dollars for the Candidate File, using an exchange rate of £1=$1.6. The Candidate File showed that the capital investment amounted to $15.8 billion (£9.9 billion) and stated that funding for some $11 billion of this total related to transport investments for which funding was already committed at the time of the bid. The elements that made up the $15.8 billion are shown within the notes to Figure 4 (the emboldened figures).

The public funding for the Games at the time of the bid

44   In May 2003 the Government and the Mayor of London agreed a memorandum of understanding which provided for a 'public sector funding package' of up to £2.375 billion to meet the costs of the Olympic and Paralympic Games (Figure 5). The Government is also to provide £1.044 billion towards the costs of 'non-Olympic' infrastructure (see paragraph 71) on the site of the Olympic Park.

4 Estimates at the time of the bid of the costs to be covered by the public sector funding package for the 2012 Games

	Candidate File estimates – 2004 prices in US $	Candidate File estimates – 2004 prices in £ sterling[2]	Outturn estimates at bid submission
	US $ million	£ million	£ million
Venues	1,132[3]	708	971
Venues legacy conversion	n/a	n/a	89
Olympic infrastructure	800[4]	500	640
Transport infrastructure	600[5]	375	466
Transport operating costs	n/a	n/a	234
Support for elite and community sport	n/a	n/a	300
Paralympics	72[6]	45	54
Other	n/a	n/a	238[7]
Total	–	–	**2,992**
Less Expected private sector funding (see Figure 6)	–	–	(738)
Total to be met from the public sector funding package	–	–	**2,254**

Sources: London 2012 Candidate File; outturn estimates taken from paper prepared by the Department for Culture, Media and Sport in September 2004

NOTES

1   n/a – not applicable as International Olympic Committee instructions on completion of Candidate City File did not request this information.

2   The costs were estimated in pounds sterling and converted into US dollars for the Candidate File, using an exchange rate of £1=$1.6.

3   This Figure includes the cost of sports venues (**$917 million**) and the International Broadcast Centre/Main Press Centre (**$215 million**) shown in the Candidate File. It does not include the cost of the Olympic Village (shown in the Candidate File as **$1,040 million**) which was expected to make use of a planned $1 billion public-private partnership.

4   The cost of Olympic infrastructure is included within the **$2,100 million** shown in the Candidate File for Olympic Park infrastructure. The total of $2,100 million also includes $1,300 million of investment in 'non-Olympic' infrastructure, which was to be covered by Exchequer funding (see paragraph 51).

5   $600 million represents the amount the Olympic Delivery Authority was expected to spend on transport infrastructure and was included within the **$11.5 billion** shown in the Candidate File for capital investment in roads and railways.

6   The $72 million shown for the Paralympic Games represents half of the total marginal cost of the Paralympics (shown as $144 million in the Candidate File). Under the Host City Contract, the state is required to fund 50 per cent of Paralympic costs, with the other 50 per cent to be funded by LOCOG.

7   Other costs include £190 million of security costs (see Figure 6).

8   This Figure does not include the costs incurred by LOCOG in staging the Games. LOCOG's estimated costs are set out in Appendix 6.

National Lottery funding

45   Unlike the other elements of the public sector funding package, the lottery funding depends on future ticket sales which are uncertain and we therefore looked at how this aspect of the funding is going to be generated.

a   **£750 million from designated Olympic lottery games**

46   Of the £1.5 billion of lottery funding for the Games, half is dependent on the success of designated Olympic lottery games. Camelot, the National Lottery operator, launched the first of these games, a scratchcard, less than a month after the Games were awarded to London[6] and has followed this with further scratchcards, interactive games, and in July 2006 the first draw-based game.

47   Returns to date have been higher than projected, with £16.3 million raised in 2005-06 compared with the forecast of £14 million. Camelot expects the amount raised by the designated Olympic lottery games to peak in the year of the Beijing Games and the two years immediately prior to the London Games. The National Lottery Commission has advised the Department that the amount of £750 million is achievable, in part because Camelot can apply to the Commission for games to be designated as Olympic.

---

6   The introduction of designated Olympic lottery games required primary legislation and, so that games could be launched more or less immediately should London's bid be successful, the Government introduced the Horserace Betting and Olympic Lottery Bill, which received Royal Assent in October 2004.

5	The public sector funding package for the 2012 Games		

Source	£ million	£ million
National Lottery		
■ Proceeds from designated Olympic lottery games – from the Olympic Lottery Distribution Fund	750	
■ Spending by the sports lottery distributors	340	
■ General lottery proceeds – from the National Lottery Distribution Fund	410	
National Lottery total		1,500
Greater London Authority – council tax precept		625
London Development Agency		250
Total		**2,375**

Source: Department for Culture, Media and Sport

NOTE

Of the £340 million from the sports lottery distributors, £50.5 million will go towards the costs of the Olympic venues. The remaining £289.5 million will be spent by the distributors on continuing support for elite athletes and coaches, facilities for elite and community use, and community programmes.

48   The Olympic lottery games are expected to reduce the money available to the other good causes[7] by diverting sales from the mainstream lottery games. As we reported previously[8], prior to the introduction of the designated games, Camelot estimated that 59 per cent (some £440 million over seven years) of the £750 million to be raised might come from players switching from existing games. This 'cannibalisation' rate varies according to the assumptions underlying the calculation but, using the same set of assumptions, the latest estimates supplied by Camelot to the National Lottery Commission are that 77 per cent (some £575 million) may be diverted from the non-Olympic good causes. The Department estimates that this represents about five per cent of the total income expected to be raised for the non-Olympic good causes in the period to 2012. Camelot aims to mitigate the effect of the designated Olympic lottery games on the returns to the other good causes by increasing ticket sales across the board.

b   £340 million from the sports lottery distributors

49   £340 million of National Lottery funding is to come via expenditure by the five sports lottery distributors[9]. Of this, £50.5 million (from Sport England) will be spent by the Olympic Delivery Authority on delivering the Games – £40 million towards the cost of the Aquatics Centre and £10.5 million on the Velopark. The distributors themselves will spend the remaining £289.5 million over a period of 12 years up to and beyond 2012, on continuing support for elite athletes and coaches, facilities for elite and community use, and community programmes.

c   £410 million from the National Lottery Distribution Fund

50   The remaining £410 million of lottery money will be derived from a change to the allocations to the non-Olympic good causes after 2009. Under the Horserace Betting and Olympic Lottery Act 2004, the Secretary of State for Culture, Media and Sport can make payments from the National Lottery Distribution Fund to the Olympic Lottery Distribution Fund, although the Department has yet to decide when the £410 million will be transferred and how the other individual good causes will be affected.

Exchequer funding

51   In addition to the public sector funding package outlined above, the Department is also co-ordinating Exchequer funding of £1.044 billion to cover the costs of 'non-Olympic' infrastructure (see paragraph 71). £405 million of this has been secured and the remainder will be sought as part of the Government's 2007 Comprehensive Spending Review.

The timing of funding

52   As well as the total amount, the timing of funding is also important so that the Olympic Delivery Authority has money available and is not delayed in taking forward its delivery programme. Early forecasts indicated that in all but one year the Authority's demand for funds was projected to exceed the supply. The Department is responsible for securing a smooth flow of funds to the Authority and to this end has formed an Olympic Funders Forum to consider and manage cashflow issues, and is currently in discussions with the Authority about the potential to re-profile funding to avoid cashflow difficulties in 2007-08.

---

7   The non-Olympic good causes are: the arts, sport, heritage, charities and voluntary groups, and health, education and environment projects.
8   *Managing National Lottery Distribution Fund balances* (HC 875, Session 2003-04).
9   Sport England, Sport Scotland, the Sports Council for Wales, the Sports Council for Northern Ireland and UK Sport.

53   To give the Olympic Delivery Authority more certainty about the flow of lottery funding, the Olympic Lottery Distributor is to make grant payments on a quarterly basis in advance. This was one of the lessons to emerge from the experience of the Millennium Dome. In determining the level of funding to be released, the Olympic Lottery Distributor will need assurance about the Olympic Delivery Authority's cashflow position and progress in delivering the Olympic programme. The Distributor will rely where posssible on existing monitoring information but has reserved the right to undertake its own work where it judges this to be necessary. Experience at the Dome underlines the importance of making payments only against proper professional certification.

Developments since London was chosen to host the Games

54   Following the choice of London to host the Games, the Department decided to review the cost estimates in the bid and in October 2005 it commissioned KPMG LLP to provide advice to inform the development of cost plans and budgets for the Games. Since then there has been a good deal of work on the budget for the Games. At the time of this report, however, consideration of the budget remained ongoing, with the Department in discussions with the Treasury.

55   As the budget setting process was not complete at the time of our work, to remain independent of the decision making we have not reviewed it in detail at this stage. However, as the Secretary of State for Culture, Media and Sport referred to in her evidence to the Culture, Media and Sport Committee on 21 November 2006, we will be reviewing the Department's work to establish the budget for the Olympic programme, with a view to reporting our findings when the budget has been finalised.

56   The Secretary of State also reported to the Culture, Media and Sport Committee that, although some offsetting savings have been identified, including from the changes to the design of the Olympic Park (see paragraph 21), overall the cost estimates for the Park have increased by some £900 million. A number of areas of uncertainty also remain which need to be resolved before the budget, including the funding, can be finalised **(Figure 6)**. The final cost figures are therefore expected to be significantly higher than the estimates at the time of the bid.

---

6   The budget for the Games – key areas of uncertainty at December 2006

Contingency provision. The cost estimates in the Candidate File included a contingency provision to cover unanticipated costs on individual projects. The Department is currently considering with the Treasury whether it would be desirable to increase the existing provision for contingency and to provide for an overall programme level contingency.

Tax. Treasury guidance states that tax costs should be included in cost estimates. At the time of the bid the tax status of the proposed Olympic Delivery Authority was undecided and the cost estimates in the Candidate File excluded provision for value added tax. The Government is currently considering tax costs as part of its wider consideration of the overall budget.

Security. The cost estimates at the time of the bid included £190 million for security, including the cost of security at the Olympic venues. However, in the light of global events, including the terrorist attacks in London on 7 July 2005, the Department expects the original provision will need to increase substantially, although the costs of the wider security measures that will be needed in London and across the UK are not included in the cost estimates for the Games.

Private sector investment. At the time of the bid it was assumed that some Olympic infrastructure and regeneration costs would be met by private sector investment or financing of around £750 million, thereby reducing the cost of the Games to the public sector. However, in the light of advice following the bid, the Department concluded there was little prospect of securing significant private sector funding to deliver the Olympic Park in view of the tight timescale for delivering the Park and the lack of an identifiable revenue stream. Private sector funding is still envisaged for the Olympic Village.

Source: National Audit Office, drawing on information from the Department for Culture, Media and Sport

---

57   It is clearly important that the budget set for the Games is robust and soundly based. However, the longer the lack of an agreed budget goes on, the greater the risk of it having an adverse impact on the Olympic programme. Although the Olympic Delivery Authority has an operating budget for the current financial year approved by the Olympic Board, without an agreed whole-life budget for the programme as a whole, the Authority is not able to finalise its lifetime corporate plan, with implications for budgetary planning and control. The Authority is therefore having to make decisions about individual projects without certainty about its overall budget and long term funding. Delay in producing a final budget could also impact on the negotiating position of those letting contracts for the Games, and on the credibility of the Olympic programme in the round and its attractiveness to potential sponsors.

58 On the funding side, at the time it was agreed in 2003 the Department anticipated that the public sector funding package for the Games would be more than sufficient. The current position on costs, however, indicates that substantial further funding is likely to be required. The Government is the ultimate guarantor of funding for the Games and, in the event of a shortfall between Olympic costs and revenues, expects to discharge that responsibility "in a sharing arrangement to be agreed as appropriate with the Mayor of London and through seeking additional National Lottery funding in amounts to be agreed at the time"[10]. It is not yet clear what this would mean in practice or what additional Exchequer funding might be available for the Games. The source of any extra funding on top of that set out in Figure 5 is also linked to whether the costs concerned are classed as 'Olympic' or 'non-Olympic' (see paragraphs 69 to 72).

LOCOG's budget for staging the Games

59 The London 2012 Candidate File also included estimated staging costs and revenues for LOCOG of £1.5 billion at 2004 prices (Appendix 6). Since London was awarded the Games, work has been ongoing to review these costs, including identifying the scope for savings and converting the figures into cash outturn prices which has produced a revised budget of around £2 billion.

60 LOCOG is expected to be self-financing over the course of its existence, although it will receive public funding in 2012 towards the cost of the Paralympic Games. LOCOG has arranged a commercial loan facility to fund its activities over the next few years because the majority of its income is not due to be received until 2011 and 2012. Any surplus LOCOG generates will be distributed to the International Olympic Committee, the British Olympic Association and to sport in the UK, while any final shortfall between LOCOG's costs and revenues will be covered by the Government's underwriting guarantee (paragraph 40).

61 The Candidate File detailed LOCOG's planned revenue sources, including estimated income from sponsorship, ticket sales and merchandising. As well as contributions from the International Olympic Committee's top sponsors, LOCOG was planning to raise around a third of its revenue from local sponsorship and during 2006 entered into discussions with possible sponsors in six sectors – automotive, banking, insurance, oil and gas, telecoms and utilities.

62 Raising sufficient sponsorship is therefore one of the main challenges that LOCOG faces and it regards protection of the Olympic brand as key to its effectiveness in this area. The London Olympic Games and Paralympic Games Act 2006 included provisions to control the use of the Olympic symbol and associated words to help make the Olympic brand valuable to sponsors so they are willing to pay to be associated with it.

63 Experience at the Millennium Dome, where the income generated fell well short of the amounts forecast, holds lessons for a number of LOCOG's planned revenue sources. The lessons, including those set out in the Comptroller and Auditor General's reports[11] on the Dome, include the following.

- On sponsorship, income at the Dome was lower and slower than expected, and working with commercial sponsors involved a good deal of management time and uncertainty over the final level of the financial contribution in terms of converting sponsorship commitments into cash.

- On ticket sales, as well as shortfalls in visitor numbers and in the income yield from each visitor, the Dome also experienced difficulties when it introduced 'on the door' ticketing arrangements, highlighting a need for strong controls, especially where cash is involved, and rigorous monitoring.

- On merchandising, the disappointing retail performance at the Dome was attributable to a number of factors, including too many product lines, too few points of sale, weaknesses in the computer system for managing the retail inventory, and a retail strategy based on maximising margin rather than sales.

Being clear about the cost of the Games to the public sector

64 Being clear about the scope of the Olympic programme and which costs are included in the public sector budget for the Games is important for effective budgetary control. For example, without defining which costs are to be allocated to which budget and applying these definitions consistently, overspending against one budget could be obscured by costs being allocated to a different budget.

---

10   Memorandum of Understanding on Olympic funding between the Government and the Mayor of London (June 2003).
11   *The Millennium Dome* (HC 936, Session 1999-2000) and *Winding-up the New Millennium Experience Company Limited* (HC 749, Session 2001-02).

65 Within the Olympic Delivery Authority, costs will need to be allocated between its Olympic and non-Olympic budgets (see paragraphs 69 to 72). Another important aspect of cost definition concerns the split of expenditure between the Authority and LOCOG since there is a risk of a grey area in terms of where in practice the Authority's responsibility for venue construction stops and LOCOG's responsibility for fitting out the venues starts. Misallocation of venue or infrastructure costs to LOCOG would worsen its financial position, while misallocation of staging costs to the Authority would mean a higher level of public funding for the Games.

66 The Olympic Delivery Authority and LOCOG are working together to manage this risk. There is a set of principles for cost allocation and both organisations are represented on the venue steering groups, which will agree detailed specifications for design and fit-out and the split of costs on a venue by venue basis.

67 It is also important to be clear about which costs will be regarded as part of routine government programmes and bid for as part of normal spending processes, and those which are expected to make a clear contribution to the Games and may be used to justify additional resources.

68 In terms of assessing the overall cost of the Games and how much public funding has been required, the costs range from those which are directly related to the Games to others where the link is less direct. While there are definitions for the 'Olympic' and 'non-Olympic' expenditure that will be incurred by the Olympic Delivery Authority, thinking more widely the Government will need to decide how to assess the overall cost of the Games, including weighing up the costs and benefits of the systems and processes needed to capture information on the wider costs. In assessing the overall cost of the Games, there are potentially four categories of relevant costs.

a **'Olympic' costs**

69 The split between Olympic and non-Olympic costs is to some extent a matter of judgement, but the Department and the Greater London Authority have agreed a definition as to which costs should be classified as Olympic and which as non-Olympic.

70 'Olympic' costs comprise expenditure by the Olympic Delivery Authority on new venues and facilities for the Games and the infrastructure associated with them. They also include the Authority's operating costs and the costs of its Delivery Partner, and the spending by the sports lottery distributors on support for elite and community sport (paragraph 49). These costs are to be met by the public sector funding package for the Games.

b **'Non-Olympic' costs**

71 'Non-Olympic' costs comprise expenditure by the Olympic Delivery Authority on ancillary infrastructure in the Olympic Park, such as the undergrounding of power lines. The definition agreed by the Department and the Greater London Authority uses the term 'non-Olympic' because it is assumed that these costs would have been incurred as part of the planned regeneration of the Lower Lea Valley in East London but have been brought forward to facilitate the delivery of the Games. 'Non-Olympic' costs are to be met by Exchequer funding.

72 There are also some projects, such as roads, bridges and tunnels, where the costs are to be allocated 75 per cent 'Olympic' and 25 per cent 'non-Olympic'.

c **Staging costs**

73 The staging costs incurred by LOCOG are not expected to be counted within the public sector budget for the Games as LOCOG is intended to be self-financing. In the event that there is a shortfall between LOCOG's costs and revenue, however, the extent to which the Government's guarantee is called upon will represent part of the cost of the Games to the public sector, as will the public funding LOCOG is expected to receive in 2012 to help cover the costs of the Paralympics.

d   Wider costs

74   In the lead-up to 2012 many government departments and other public bodies will dedicate staff to Olympic related work and this expenditure may be considered as part of the cost of the Games. The running costs of the Government Olympic Executive, for example, are expected to be some £3 million a year.

75   The scale of the Olympic programme means that a range of central and local government bodies will also incur costs that are to some extent associated with the Games, such as the costs of improving transport links, of policing London during the event, and of providing health services in the local area. Such activities fall within the scope of pre-existing programmes and will be subject to the usual public spending and accountability arrangements at either national or local level. The activities will, however, be essential to the success of the Games and spending may be brought forward or be higher than it would otherwise have been.

The need for strong financial management and control

76   The need for strong financial management and control on the Olympic programme is plain. The Olympic Delivery Authority and LOCOG have in place professional Finance Directors, and the Authority is in the process of establishing four financial services panels for the provision of financial and accountancy advice.

77   The experience of the Millennium Dome reinforces the importance of effective financial management and control from the outset. In his reports on the Dome, the Comptroller and Auditor General noted weaknesses in financial management, including concerns about the quality of financial control and forecasting. Particular lessons are:

■   the need to maintain comprehensive and accurate asset registers, which will help with the transfer of asset ownership at the end of the programme. At the Dome, disposing of assets was made more costly and complicated by the absence of detailed records; and

■   the need for strong contract management arrangements, with comprehensive contract records and payments made only in accordance with certified work carried out. At the Dome, the absence of adequate records made it difficult to track contractual commitments and liabilities.

RISK AREA 3

The requirement for the budget to be clearly determined and managed effectively – action required to manage risk

a   Setting a budget for the Games and making clear how this will be funded.

b   Being clear how the cashflow needs of the Olympic Delivery Authority will be met.

c   Making clear how the £410 million of funding from the National Lottery Distribution Fund will be derived as this will impact on the other good causes.

d   Securing LOCOG's income, including turning sponsorship pledges into cash.

e   Being clear about what costs are associated with delivering the Games and capturing these costs on a consistent basis. Key aspects will be:

■   within the Olympic Delivery Authority, applying the Olympic/non-Olympic definitions consistently;

■   being clear for each project where the boundaries lie between construction (the Olympic Delivery Authority's responsibility) and fit-out (LOCOG's responsibility); and

■   deciding what costs would be counted in any final reckoning of what the Games have cost, being clear about these throughout, and ensuring principles and processes are in place to support accurate reporting.

f   Exercising effective oversight of the Olympic Delivery Authority and LOCOG as their financial position will determine directly whether, and if so to what extent, the Government's underwriting guarantee will be called upon.

Risk area 4: Applying effective procurement practices

78   The Olympic delivery programme will involve extensive procurement activity in the coming years and the Olympic Delivery Authority has already carried out two major procurement exercises.

■   In July 2006 the Olympic Delivery Authority began the competitive process to procure an integrated team to undertake the design, planning and construction work for the main Olympic Stadium. The Authority began negotiations with the preferred team in October 2006 and hopes to confirm the appointment in January 2007.

■   In September 2006, following a two-stage competitive process, the Olympic Delivery Authority appointed the CLM Consortium as its Delivery Partner to provide support in managing the delivery of the Olympic venues and infrastructure. The Delivery Partner is expected to supplement the Authority's own resources by bringing construction and programme management expertise and experience of previous Games and other large scale construction projects.

79   In total the Olympic Delivery Authority is expected to spend over £3 billion on goods, services and works, and from 2009 LOCOG's procurement programme for goods and services for the Games themselves will begin in earnest. Strong procurement practices will be needed to achieve value for money, ensure that contracts are awarded in an open and fair way in line with best practice, and to demonstrate that this is the case.

80   Members of the Olympic Delivery Authority's Board and management team have procurement experience, and more widely the Authority is tapping into the experience and expertise available on procurement matters across government. For example, to help ensure the procurement for the Delivery Partner was in line with best practice, the process was overseen by an advisory 'compliance and oversight group' of external procurement experts.

81   In July 2006 the Olympic Delivery Authority published a draft procurement policy for consultation. The policy, which was developed with help from the Office of Government Commerce and others, will guide the way in which the Authority carries out its procurement, and will be supported by more detailed procedures and working instructions. The consultation process ran until October 2006, and the policy will now be revisited and reissued.

82   The Olympic Delivery Authority subscribes to best practice as codified by the Office of Government Commerce, for example in its guidance on 'Achieving excellence in construction procurement'. In July 2006 the Authority was also among the signatories to the '2012 Construction Commitments', which were developed by a Task Group of the Strategic Forum for Construction[12], in conjunction with the Department for Culture, Media and Sport and the Department for Trade and Industry, to demonstrate and develop good practice in the UK construction industry.

83   The Construction Commitments are designed to promote collaborative working and ensure the successful delivery of the Games infrastructure, buildings and subsequent legacy. They set out good practice principles in six areas of the construction process (client leadership; procurement and integration; design; sustainability; commitment to people; and health and safety) and provide a helpful framework to guide the construction programme for the 2012 Games, including approaches set out in the Comptroller and Auditor General's report on 'Improving public services through better construction'[13].

RISK AREA 4

Applying effective procurement practices – action required to manage risk

a   Being clear about the respective roles and responsibilities of the Olympic Delivery Authority and its Delivery Partner, and ensuring that the arrangement enables the Authority to contain its operating costs as planned.

b   Achieving confidence in the approach to procurement by awarding contracts in an open and fair way, and applying best practice including that set out in the procurement policy and the Construction Commitments. Any departures from best practice required to deliver the Games to time and cost should be clear and explicit at the time.

12   The Strategic Forum for Construction is an industry body, funded by the Department for Trade and Industry.
13   *Improving public services through better construction* (HC 364, Session 2004-05).

Risk area 5: Planning for a lasting legacy

84 The prospect of the legacy that hosting the Olympic and Paralympic Games would bring was a key element of London's bid. Legacy can be viewed in terms of the venues that will remain after 2012, the regeneration of the local area, and also the wider benefits that the Games are expected to bring to London and the UK more generally.

Venues

85 The London 2012 Candidate File outlined legacy proposals for the five new sports venues that will remain on the Olympic Park site following the Games, including the main Stadium and the Aquatics Centre. Developing more detailed plans is the responsibility of the project groups for each venue, involving representatives from the Olympic Delivery Authority, LOCOG and other stakeholders, whose work is overseen by an over-arching venue legacy group. Key questions to be resolved are who will own the individual venues after the Games, who will cover conversion and running costs, and the extent to which the venues will be available for sporting use by local communities, which in itself would help to ensure the venues are well maintained.

86 Overall responsibility for delivering agreed sustainable legacy plans for the Olympic Park and venues, and for converting the venues for legacy use, rests with the Olympic Delivery Authority. Although final plans have not yet been agreed, from our discussions with the Authority and other stakeholders, it was clear that providing for legacy is central to their thinking on design and construction. The design of a venue has an impact not just on the construction costs but also on maintenance and operating costs in the longer term. On the Aquatics Centre, for example, the proposed design has been revisited, in part because of concerns about the affordability of operating costs after 2012.

87 The London 2012 Candidate File also proposed the creation of a London Olympic Institute on the site of the Olympic Park, which would provide facilities and services for elite athletes, as well as encouraging participation in sport. The British Olympic Association is responsible for delivering the Institute in a viable form and is currently developing its plans in consultation with sporting stakeholders. A consideration will be how the Institute fits with the English Institute of Sport and other support for elite athletes funded by UK Sport.

Regeneration of the local area

88 The majority of the venues for the Games fall within five London Boroughs – Greenwich, Hackney, Newham, Tower Hamlets and Waltham Forest. The Olympic Park itself is located mainly in Newham and the Games are seen as a major opportunity to help regenerate one of the poorest and most disadvantaged parts of the UK. The site also falls within the Thames Gateway, one of the Government's regeneration priorities, and the Games are expected to help achieve the aims of that programme.

89 The aim is for the local area to benefit from improved transport links and other infrastructure, and the Olympic Park itself will become new urban parkland. In terms of housing, the Olympic Village is expected to be converted into 3,600 apartments after the Games, and the London Development Agency has estimated that a total of 9,000 new homes will ultimately be available in the Olympic Park. As well as the jobs relating to the construction and staging of the Games, 12,000 jobs are expected to be created from the legacy development of the Olympic Park area.

Wider benefits

90 One of the objectives for the Games is to maximise the economic, social, health and environmental benefits of the Games for the UK, particularly through regeneration and sustainable development in East London. This objective has been broken down into two sets of mirroring sub-objectives (see Appendix 5), for the Government in relation to the UK as a whole and for the Mayor in relation to London.

91 Work to turn each of the sub-objectives into detailed delivery plans is ongoing, with, at national level, the work being led by one or more government departments, in conjunction with other relevant stakeholders. A parallel process is also going on at London level, and the aim was to have the delivery plans in place by the end of 2006. At both national and local level, the intention is that the delivery plans will build on existing objectives and priorities, with bodies identifying how they can use the Games as a catalyst to deliver or add value to their mainstream programmes.

92 LOCOG's Nations and Regions Group has been set up to help engage the whole of the UK with the 2012 Games and deliver a nationwide legacy. The Group has 12 members, representing Scotland, Wales, Northern Ireland and each of the nine English regions. Each member of the Group chairs a working group in their nation or region, whose membership includes representatives from sport, business, local government, tourism, education, the voluntary sector and other key interest groups. The working groups are currently developing strategies aimed at ensuring the impact of the Games is spread across the country.

RISK AREA 5

Planning for a lasting legacy – action required to manage risk

a   Developing robust business plans for the Olympic venues with a clear focus on whole-life costs, to avoid the risk of facilities being under-used or unaffordable after the Games.

b   Agreeing who will be responsible for each facility during the transition phase after the Games, who will cover conversion and ongoing running costs, and who will own the assets in their legacy form.

c   Looking beyond the venues, identifying the key legacy benefits that it is realistic to expect from the Games, and where possible quantifying these so that it will be clear whether they have been achieved.

d   Embedding the development of delivery plans into normal business planning cycles so they become a meaningful part of the core processes of the departments and other bodies involved.

e   Deciding what benefits would be counted in any final reckoning of the costs and benefits of the Games, being clear about these throughout, and ensuring principles and processes are in place to support accurate reporting.

f   Ensuring that in any final reckoning, costs and benefits are approached in the same way so that, for example, any assessment of wider benefits is not set against a narrow definition of cost.

g   Ensuring the legacy proposals for the Olympic Park are integrated with the plans for the wider Thames Gateway and surrounding area.

Risk area 6: The installation of effective progress monitoring and risk management arrangements

93   Effective progress monitoring and risk management will be essential to the successful delivery of the Olympic programme, with its multiple stakeholders, many individual projects, variety of commitments made to the International Olympic Committee, and inherent interdependencies in delivering the programme as a whole. The Olympic Board has a key role in this regard, supported by the Olympic Board Steering Group and the Olympic Programme Support Unit.

94   The Olympic Programme Support Unit has a pivotal role in working with stakeholders to track the overall health of the programme so that the Olympic Board and the Steering Group have the right information available at the right time, and are well placed to make decisions for the benefit of the programme as a whole. The flow of information is illustrated in **Figure 7**.

95   The Olympic Programme Support Unit is answerable to the Olympic Board and the Steering Group collectively. The Unit is expected to cost around £1 million a year and, as the Olympic Lottery Distributor decided in May 2006 not to provide lottery funding at that time, the Unit has been funded by the Department, funding that is additional to the cost of the Government Olympic Executive (paragraph 34). In August 2006 the Department, the Greater London Authority and LOCOG agreed to share equally the costs of the Unit with backdated effect from the start of 2006-07.

96   By September 2006 the Olympic Programme Support Unit had built up its capacity to eight staff, including a Director. Several stakeholders commented on the benefits of the Unit being co-located with the Olympic Delivery Authority and LOCOG in helping it to develop its own comprehensive and independent view of progress and issues across the programme.

Progress reporting

97   The Olympic programme objectives and sub-objectives (Appendix 5) provide the framework for progress reporting. Each stakeholder is to provide the Olympic Programme Support Unit with a monthly report on developments, which the Unit uses to provide condensed over-arching reports to the Olympic Board and the Steering Group.

98   The lead stakeholders for each sub-objective are developing delivery plans which will outline how the sub-objective will be achieved in more detail and include outcomes, measures, and milestones. Once these plans have been agreed, the Olympic Programme Support Unit will be able to compare and challenge monthly progress reports against a baseline.

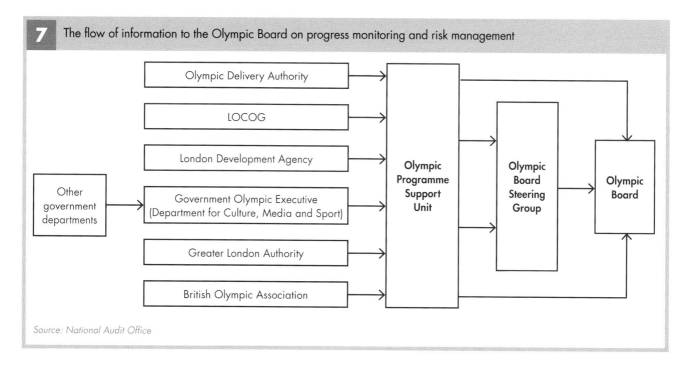

7 The flow of information to the Olympic Board on progress monitoring and risk management

Source: National Audit Office

99 The Olympic Programme Support Unit relies on the Government Olympic Executive within the Department for Culture, Media and Sport for information on central government's contribution to the programme, which includes the delivery of commitments made in respect of, for example, transport improvements, security and health care, on which a successful Games will in part depend.

Risk management

100 Stakeholders are at different stages in developing their own risk strategies and registers to identify and manage the risks specific to delivering their responsibilities. At a programme level, the Olympic Programme Support Unit is responsible for collating an 'issues and risks' register, based on information provided by the stakeholders about their own issues and risks. The Unit judges which of these risks should be brought to the attention of the Olympic Board and the Steering Group, and is working with the Steering Group on clarifying the criteria for exercising these judgements. There is also recognition of the need for a 'top down' view of key strategic and political risks, and the Steering Group held its first strategic risk workshop in October 2006.

RISK AREA 6

The installation of effective progress monitoring and risk management arrangements – action required to manage risk

a   Completing work to put in place progress monitoring and risk management arrangements, for individual organisations and the programme as a whole.

b   Maintaining the pivotal role of the Olympic Programme Support Unit in providing independent advice and assurance on the programme, a role which goes beyond scrutinising information received and also involves active engagement with the key stakeholders.

APPENDIX ONE

Background facts about the London 2012 Olympic and Paralympic Games

- Nine cities originally submitted applications to host the 2012 Games – Havana, Istanbul, Leipzig, London, Madrid, Moscow, New York, Paris and Rio de Janeiro.

- In May 2004 the International Olympic Committee's Executive Board narrowed the applications down to five Candidate Cities – London, Madrid, Moscow, New York and Paris.

- Following four rounds of voting in Singapore on 6 July 2005, London was chosen to host the 2012 Games by taking 54 International Olympic Committee Member votes out of a possible 104. There were 2,578 days, just over seven years, to go before the opening ceremony of the Olympic Games on 27 July 2012.

- Developing the Olympic Park site will involve:

  - 3,000 metres of river and 3,800 metres of canal being dredged;

  - 3 million cubic metres of soil being cleaned and moved;

  - about 10 kilometres of new roads being laid; and

  - over 150,000 seats being installed in venues.

- Ten railway lines will serve the Olympic Park with a train expected to arrive, on average, every 15 seconds at peak times.

- The newly built venues in the Olympic Park will include the Olympic Stadium, Aquatics Centre, Velopark, Hockey Centre, Paralympic tennis and archery facility, and arenas to stage basketball, fencing, modern pentathlon and handball.

- There are a further 18 existing venues which will be used for various events. These are mostly in and around London, but also include six football stadiums around Britain, rowing at Eton Dorney, canoe slalom at Broxbourne and sailing at Weymouth and Portland.

- Around 40 'test events' will be held at the venues in advance of the Games.

- Around 8 million tickets will be available for the Olympic Games, with another 1.6 million for the Paralympic Games.

- Up to 70,000 volunteers will be sought to help with running the Games.

- London is expected to be host to over 23,000 competitors and officials from more than 200 countries.

- 299 gold medals will be awarded in 26 sports at the Olympic Games, and 538 gold medals will be awarded in 19 sports at the Paralympic Games.

Sources: information published by LOCOG, the Olympic Delivery Authority, and the International Olympic Committee

APPENDIX TWO

Study methods

1   This report is our first about the preparations for the London 2012 Olympic and Paralympic Games. It considers the progress that has been made since July 2005 when the International Olympic Committee chose London as the host city for 2012, and identifies key risks and challenges going forward. In particular we considered progress in developing the organisational and governance framework and the cost and revenue forecasts for the Games.

2   The report does not cover the steps being taken to support elite athletes with a view to securing success at the London 2012 Olympic and Paralympic Games or to use the Games to help increase sports participation at community and grassroots level.

Review of key documents and other papers

3   We examined key legal and financial documents put in place to define and manage the roles and relationships of the various organisations involved in delivering and funding the London 2012 Games, and related departmental papers. Our work was designed to establish in particular:

■   the responsibilities and accountabilities of the various bodies involved in the Games;

■   the arrangements for inter-agency working and decision making; and

■   the arrangements for funding the Games.

Key documents we examined

■   Memorandum of Understanding on Olympic funding between the Government and the Mayor of London (June 2003).

■   Horserace Betting and Olympic Lottery Act 2004.

■   The London 2012 Candidate File and associated guarantees submitted to the International Olympic Committee (November 2004).

■   Olympic Games and Paralympic Games 2012: Arrangements relating to the Undertaking and Candidature File (November 2004). *This is a memorandum of understanding between the Secretary of State for Culture, Media and Sport, the Mayor of London and the British Olympic Association.*

■   Olympic Staging Structure: Master Framework Memorandum (February 2005). *This is a further memorandum of understanding between the Secretary of State for Culture, Media and Sport, the Mayor of London and the British Olympic Association.*

■   Joint Venture Agreement relating to the establishment and operation of the London Organising Committee of the Olympic Games Limited (LOCOG) (February 2005). *This is an agreement between the Secretary of State for Culture, Media and Sport, the Mayor of London and the British Olympic Association.*

■   Host City Contract between the International Olympic Committee, the Mayor of London and the British Olympic Association (July 2005). *LOCOG also became a party to the Contract once it had been formally established.*

■   London Olympic Games and Paralympic Games Act 2006.

■   Olympic Delivery Authority Management Statement and Financial Memorandum (July 2006).

4 We also examined the January 2003 report by the Culture, Media and Sport Committee 'A London Olympic bid for all' (Third Report of Session 2002-03, HC 268), submissions made by the Department and others to inform the Committee's inquiry, and the Government's response to the Committee's report.

Review of the cost and revenue estimates for the Games

5 As the budget setting process was not complete at the time of our work, to remain independent of the decision making we did not review the cost estimates in detail at this stage. We did, however, review cost definitions, including which costs are to be treated as 'Olympic' and which 'non-Olympic'.

6 We reviewed the various funding streams for the Games. We examined the funding agreement between the Department and the Mayor of London, National Lottery Commission papers relating to the funding to be raised by the designated Olympic lottery games, and the contingent liabilities that the Government has notified to Parliament. We also reviewed papers relating to the Olympic Delivery Authority's cashflow and the terms of reference for the Olympic Funders Forum.

Interviews at the Department for Culture, Media and Sport

7 We carried out a series of interviews with the Chief Executive and other senior staff in the Government Olympic Executive at the Department for Culture, Media and Sport. The interviews covered:

- progress to date in the preparations for the Games;
- the development of delivery structures and governance arrangements;
- arrangements for inter-agency working and decision making;
- the development of cost and revenue estimates;
- plans for delivering legacy benefits;
- arrangements for progress monitoring and risk management;
- arrangements for cross-government co-ordination;
- lessons from previous Olympic and Paralympic Games; and
- the role of the Government Olympic Executive.

8 We also met with the team responsible for internal audit at the Department to discuss our respective work on matters relating to the London 2012 Games.

Interviews with other stakeholders

9 We carried out interviews with senior staff at organisations with a role in delivering the Games. The interviews were designed to get views on:

- the responsibilities and accountabilities of the various bodies involved in delivering the Games;
- arrangements for inter-agency working and decision making;
- the cost and revenue estimates for the Games;
- progress monitoring and risk management; and
- plans for delivering legacy benefits.

The people and organisations we interviewed

- British Olympic Association (Chief Executive and other staff).
- British Paralympic Association (Chief Executive).
- Greater London Authority (Policy Director to the Mayor of London, Executive Director of Finance and Performance, and other staff).
- HM Treasury (Team Leader, Devolved Countries and the Regions, and other staff).
- London Borough of Newham (Mayor of Newham and other staff).
- London Development Agency (Director of Finance).
- London Organising Committee of the Olympic Games and Paralympic Games (Chief Executive, Chief Operating Officer and Finance Director).
- National Lottery Commission (Chief Executive and other staff).
- Office of Government Commerce (Director of Mission Critical Engagement and other staff).
- Olympic Delivery Authority (Chairman, Chair of the Audit Committee, Chief Executive, Finance Director and other staff).
- Olympic Lottery Distributor (Interim Chief Executive and other staff).
- Olympic Programme Support Unit (Director).
- Sport England (Interim Chief Executive).

Audit reports relating to the costs of Olympic and Paralympic Games

- The Sydney 2000 Olympic and Paralympic Games – Review of Estimates (Report by the Audit Office of New South Wales, 1999).
- Cost of the Olympic and Paralympic Games (Report to Parliament by the Auditor General of New South Wales, 2002).
- Review of Estimates Related to Vancouver's Bid to Stage the 2012 Olympic Winter Games and Paralympic Winter Games (Report by the Office of the Auditor General of British Columbia, 2003).
- The 2012 Olympic and Paralympic Winter Games: Review of Estimates Related to the Provinces (Report by the Office of the Auditor General of British Columbia, 2006).

13 We met with representatives of the Chinese National Audit Office to discuss the Beijing Games, and have arranged with the Auditor General in China to learn lessons from 2008 that could be usefully applied to London.

14 We also met with senior staff from the Sydney Organising Committee for the Olympic Games and the Olympic Co-ordination Authority, to discuss Sydney's experience of hosting the Games and lessons that could be applied to London.

10 We also met Derek Wyatt MP, Chair of the All-Party Parliamentary Olympic and Paralympic Group, to discuss matters relating to the London 2012 Games.

International comparisons

11 Our work was informed by the experience of other host cities, including Sydney and Athens (which hosted the Summer Games in 2000 and 2004 respectively), Beijing (which is preparing to host the Summer Games in 2008), and Vancouver (which is to host the Winter Games in 2010).

12 We reviewed audit reports on these Games and in particular drew upon reports relating to costs.

APPENDIX THREE

Location of the Olympic venues and the design of the Olympic Park

Appendix 3 overleaf

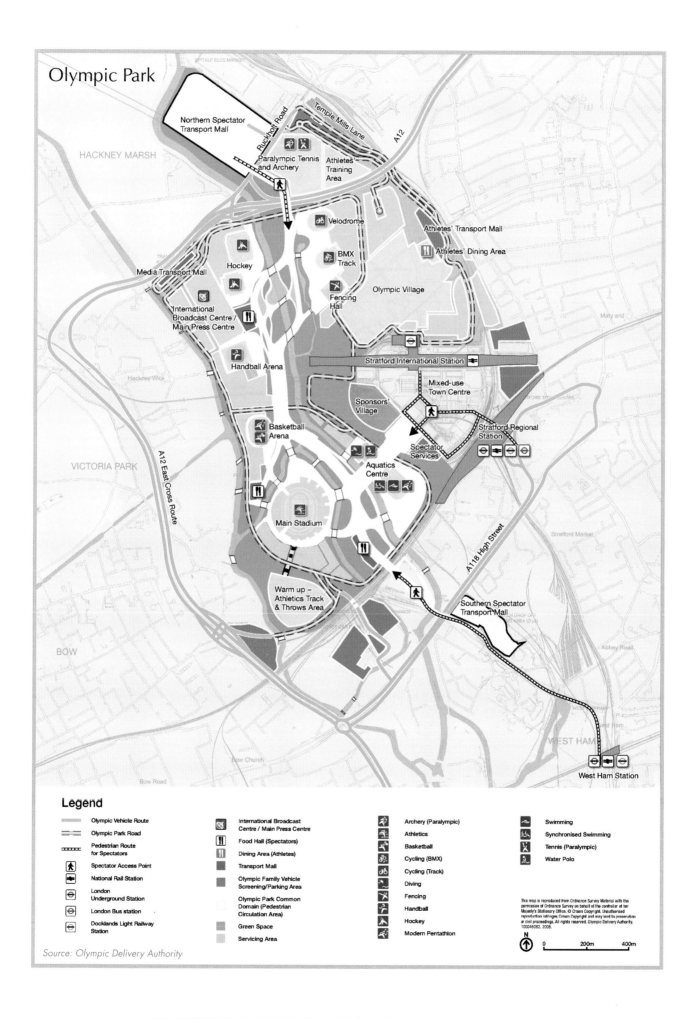

Olympic Park

Legend

	Olympic Vehicle Route
	Olympic Park Road
	Pedestrian Route for Spectators
	Spectator Access Point
	National Rail Station
	London Underground Station
	London Bus station
	Docklands Light Railway Station

	International Broadcast Centre / Main Press Centre
	Food Hall (Spectators)
	Dining Area (Athletes)
	Transport Mall
	Olympic Family Vehicle Screening/Parking Area
	Olympic Park Common Domain (Pedestrian Circulation Area)
	Green Space
	Servicing Area

	Archery (Paralympic)
	Athletics
	Basketball
	Cycling (BMX)
	Cycling (Track)
	Diving
	Fencing
	Handball
	Hockey
	Modern Pentathlon

	Swimming
	Synchronised Swimming
	Tennis (Paralympic)
	Water Polo

This map is reproduced from Ordnance Survey Material with the permission of Ordnance Survey on behalf of the controller of her Majesty's Stationery Office. © Crown Copyright. Unauthorised reproduction infringes Crown Copyright and may lead to prosecution or civil proceedings. All rights reserved. Olympic Delivery Authority. 100046082, 2008.

N
0   200m   400m

Source: Olympic Delivery Authority

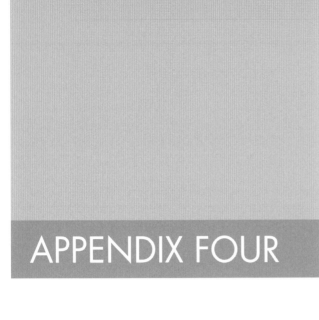

APPENDIX FOUR

Key organisations and groups involved in the delivery of the London 2012 Olympic and Paralympic Games

This Appendix sets out details of the key organisations and groups involved in delivering and funding the London 2012 Games from the perspective of this report; they are shown in alphabetical order.

Organisation/group	Background	Role in relation to the London 2012 Games
British Olympic Association	■ The National Olympic Committee for Great Britain and Northern Ireland.	■ Co-signatory to the Host City Contract, signed with the International Olympic Committee. ■ Co-signatory to the joint venture agreement which established LOCOG. ■ The Chair is a member of the Olympic Board. ■ Represented on LOCOG's Board, the Olympic Board Steering Group and other stakeholder groups.
British Paralympic Association	■ The National Paralympic Committee for Great Britain and Northern Ireland.	■ Represented on LOCOG's Board, the Olympic Board Steering Group and other stakeholder groups.
Camelot Group plc	■ Private sector operator of the National Lottery, under a licence which runs to 2009.	■ Runs the National Lottery games which raise funding for the good causes, including the Olympic and Paralympic Games.
CLM Consortium	■ Consortium of three companies – CH2M HILL, Laing O'Rourke and Mace.	■ As the Olympic Delivery Authority's Delivery Partner, will support in project managing the delivery programme for the Olympic venues and infrastructure.
Department for Culture, Media and Sport	■ Government department.	■ The lead government department for the Games, with over-arching responsibility for managing the Government's interests and responsibilities. ■ Co-ordinating £1.044 billion of Exchequer funding towards the costs of 'non-Olympic' infrastructure (see paragraph 71). ■ Oversees the public bodies involved in the Games, including the Olympic Delivery Authority, LOCOG, the Olympic Lottery Distributor and Sport England. ■ The Secretary of State for Culture, Media and Sport is a member of the Olympic Board. ■ The Secretary of State for Culture, Media and Sport is a co-signatory to the joint venture agreement which established LOCOG. ■ The approval of the Secretary of State for Culture, Media and Sport is required for projects above the Olympic Delivery Authority's financial delegation limit of £20 million or which are deemed "novel or contentious".

Organisation/group	Background	Role in relation to the London 2012 Games
Government Olympic Executive	▪ Dedicated unit within the Department for Culture, Media and Sport.	▪ The team responsible for handling Olympic matters within the Department for Culture, Media and Sport. ▪ The Chief Executive was designated as the Accounting Officer for the Games.
Greater London Authority	▪ Strategic governing body for London covering transport, policing, fire and emergency services, economic development, planning, culture and the environment. ▪ Comprises the Mayor of London (the Executive of the Authority) and the London Assembly which scrutinises the Mayor's activities.	▪ Contributing up to £625 million to the public sector funding package for the Games, raised via a council tax precept. ▪ The Mayor of London is a co-signatory to the Host City Contract, signed with the International Olympic Committee. ▪ The Mayor of London is a member of the Olympic Board. ▪ The Mayor of London is a co-signatory to the joint venture agreement which established LOCOG. ▪ The approval of the Mayor of London is required for projects above the Olympic Delivery Authority's financial delegation limit of £20 million or which are deemed "novel or contentious".
HM Treasury	▪ Government department.	▪ Involved in discussions about the cost estimates and funding for the Games. ▪ Treasury approval is required for projects above the Olympic Delivery Authority's financial delegation limit of £20 million or which are deemed "novel or contentious".
Inter-Departmental Steering Group	▪ Comprises senior officials from all government departments, the devolved administrations, and the Greater London Authority, and representatives from the Regional Development Agencies and Government Offices for the regions of England. ▪ Chaired by the Government Olympic Executive.	▪ Sets the strategic direction for the Government's contribution to the Games. ▪ Accountable for timely progress to deliver the Government's Olympic objectives. ▪ Identifies and manages risks to the delivery of the Government's interests and responsibilities.
International Olympic Committee	▪ International non-governmental organisation and creator of the Olympic Movement. Its primary responsibility is to supervise the organisation of the Summer and Winter Olympic Games.	▪ Elected London as the host city for 2012 in July 2005. ▪ Has Host City Contract with the Mayor of London, the British Olympic Association and LOCOG to deliver the Games as planned, or as amended by mutual agreement.
London Development Agency	▪ The Regional Development Agency for London, co-ordinating economic development and regeneration. ▪ Accountable to the Mayor of London.	▪ Responsible for acquiring the land on the Olympic Park site. ▪ Contributing up to £250 million to the public sector funding package for the Games, in addition to funding the land acquisition. ▪ Aims to maximise the opportunities to support London businesses and people into jobs, contracts and training arising from the Games and their legacy.

Organisation/group	Background	Role in relation to the London 2012 Games
London Organising Committee of the Olympic Games and Paralympic Games (LOCOG)	■ Company limited by guarantee, and a body within the central government sector, established by a joint venture agreement between the Secretary of State for Culture, Media and Sport, the Mayor of London and the British Olympic Association. Within central government LOCOG is overseen by the Department for Culture, Media and Sport.	■ Responsible for the operational and staging aspects of the Games. ■ The liaison point for the International Olympic Committee and a party to the Host City Contract, signed with the International Olympic Committee. ■ The Chair of LOCOG is a member of the Olympic Board.
MISC 25	■ The Ministerial Committee on Olympic and Paralympic Games. ■ Chaired by the current Leader of the House of Commons, and other Members include the Secretary of State for Culture, Media and Sport, the Deputy Prime Minister, and other Secretaries of State and Ministers of State.	■ Co-ordinates and oversees Government issues relating to the Games.
National Lottery Commission	■ Non-departmental public body, sponsored by the Department for Culture, Media and Sport.	■ Regulates the National Lottery, including considering applications from Camelot Group plc for new lottery games to be designated as 'Olympic'.
Nations and Regions Group	■ Group comprising 12 members representing Scotland, Wales, Northern Ireland and the nine English regions. The Group also involves representatives from the Department for Culture, Media and Sport, the Olympic Delivery Authority, VisitBritain, the Local Government Association and the British Olympic Association. ■ Chaired by a LOCOG Board Member.	■ To help engage the whole of the UK with the 2012 Games and deliver a nationwide legacy.
Office of Government Commerce	■ Independent office of HM Treasury, which works with public sector organisations to help them achieve efficiency, value for money in commercial activities, and improved success from programmes and projects.	■ Conducts Gateway Reviews of procurement, major projects and programme management.
Olympic Board	■ Established by a memorandum of understanding between the Secretary of State for Culture, Media and Sport, the Mayor of London and the British Olympic Association. ■ Comprises the Secretary of State for Culture, Media and Sport, the Mayor of London, and the Chairs of the British Olympic Association and LOCOG. The Chair of the Olympic Delivery Authority attends Board meetings as a non-voting member. ■ Chaired alternately by the Secretary of State for Culture, Media and Sport and the Mayor of London.	■ Responsible for resolving and determining issues raised by members of the Olympic Board to ensure the delivery of the Games, and for ensuring that a sustainable legacy is achieved following the staging of the Games. ■ Oversees the Olympic programme, and receives reports and plans from the bodies involved in staging the Games.

Organisation/group	Background	Role in relation to the London 2012 Games
Olympic Board Steering Group	■ Comprises senior officials from the Government Olympic Executive, the Greater London Authority, the British Olympic Association, LOCOG, the Olympic Delivery Authority, the Olympic Lottery Distributor, the Department for Communities and Local Government, the British Paralympic Association and the Olympic Programme Support Unit. ■ Chaired by the Chief Executive of the Government Olympic Executive.	■ Supports the Olympic Board at official level. ■ Takes a strategic overview of the work of the stakeholders in relation to the Olympic programme as a whole. ■ Responsible for ensuring that the Olympic Board is kept informed and regularly briefed on all relevant matters.
Olympic Co-ordinators Group	■ Sits below the Inter-Departmental Steering Group and reports to it. ■ Comprises officials from across government.	■ Considers operational aspects of cross-departmental Olympic matters.
Olympic Delivery Authority	■ Established by the London Olympic and Paralympic Games Act 2006. ■ Non-departmental public body, sponsored by the Department for Culture, Media and Sport.	■ Will prepare the Olympic Park site, build the new venues and provide for their legacy use, and deliver the Olympic Village, media facilities, and infrastructure for the Games. ■ The planning authority for the Olympic Park area – any application relating to land within the area is considered by the Olympic Delivery Authority's Planning Committee rather than the local borough. ■ Responsible for developing an Olympic transport plan and for delivering Olympic transport projects.
Olympic Funders Forum	■ Working group of officials from the bodies providing public funding for the Games.	■ Considers cashflow issues with a view to ensuring the Olympic Delivery Authority has the funds it needs.
Olympic Lottery Distributor	■ Established by the Horserace Betting and Olympic Lottery Act 2004. ■ Non-departmental public body, sponsored by the Department for Culture, Media and Sport.	■ Draws down from the Olympic Lottery Distribution Fund funds raised for the Olympics and Paralympics by the designated Olympic lottery games, and from 2009 from the proceeds of mainstream National Lottery games. ■ Awards funding to projects which it considers are "necessary or expedient" for hosting the Games. The funding will go principally to the Olympic Delivery Authority but the Distributor is not precluded from funding other bodies.
Olympic Programme Support Unit	■ A dedicated unit to support the Olympic Board and the Olympic Board Steering Group. ■ To be funded jointly by the Department for Culture, Media and Sport, the Greater London Authority and LOCOG.	■ Responsible for tracking the overall health of the Olympic programme and providing reports to the Olympic Board and the Olympic Board Steering Group. ■ Provides a secretariat function to the Olympic Board and the Olympic Board Steering Group.

Organisation/group	Background	Role in relation to the London 2012 Games
Olympic Projects Review Group	■ Working group of officials including from the Government Olympic Executive, HM Treasury, the Greater London Authority, LOCOG, the Office of Government Commerce, the Olympic Delivery Authority and the Olympic Lottery Distributor. ■ Chaired by the Government Olympic Executive.	■ Assesses whether projects over the Olympic Delivery Authority's financial delegation limit of £20 million or which are deemed "novel or contentious" can be recommended to the Secretary of State for Culture, Media and Sport, the Treasury and the Mayor of London for financial approval.
Sport England	■ Non-departmental public body, sponsored by the Department for Culture, Media and Sport. ■ Provides leadership for community sport in England and distributes National Lottery funding.	■ Contributing £50.5 million of National Lottery funding to the Olympic Delivery Authority towards the costs of the Aquatics Centre (£40 million) and Velopark (£10.5 million). ■ Along with the other sports lottery distributors (Sport Scotland, the Sports Council for Northern Ireland, the Sports Council for Wales and UK Sport), will spend £289.5 million of the public sector funding package for the Games on elite and community sport.
Strategic Forum for Construction	■ Industry body funded by the Department for Trade and Industry.	■ Developed the '2012 Construction Commitments', in conjunction with the Department for Culture, Media and Sport and the Department for Trade and Industry. The Commitments set out good practice principles to guide the construction programme for the Games.
Transport for London	■ Responsible for London's transport system. ■ Chaired by and accountable to the Mayor of London.	■ Delivery of transport infrastructure improvements in London. ■ Works with the Olympic Delivery Authority to develop transport plans for the Games.

APPENDIX FIVE

Olympic and Paralympic Games programme objectives

Strategic objective	Lead stakeholder		Sub-objective
1 To stage an inspirational Olympic Games and Paralympic Games for the athletes, the Olympic Family and the viewing public	LOCOG	1.1	Deliver an inspirational environment and experience for athletes and provide a first class experience for the Olympic Family and spectators
	LOCOG	1.2	Meet International Olympic Committee and International Paralympic Committee needs and specifications, including venue overlays
	LOCOG	1.3	Ensure effective and efficient planning and operation of the Olympic and Paralympic Games (including security, transport, technology, health, volunteering and accessibility)
	LOCOG	1.4	Maximise audience size at venues
	LOCOG	1.5	Secure support and engagement across all sections of the UK public
	LOCOG	1.6	Deliver effective media presentation and maximise global audience size
	LOCOG	1.7	Communicate Olympic values across the world, particularly amongst young people
	LOCOG	1.8	Stage inspiring ceremonies and cultural events
	LOCOG	1.9	Deliver an operating surplus from the Olympic Games and Paralympic Games
	LOCOG	1.10	Operate sustainable and environmentally responsible Olympic Games and Paralympic Games
2 To deliver the Olympic Park and all venues on time, within agreed budget and to specification, minimising the call on public funds and providing for a sustainable legacy	London Development Agency	2.1	Assemble and remediate land for Games venues
	Olympic Delivery Authority	2.2	Create infrastructure and facilities associated with Games venues to time and agreed budget in accordance with principles of sustainable development
	Olympic Delivery Authority	2.3	Deliver Olympic and Paralympic venues to time, to design and building specification and to agreed budget, providing for agreed legacy use
	Department for Culture, Media and Sport	2.4	Secure smooth flow of public funds to the Olympic Delivery Authority
	Olympic Delivery Authority	2.5	Deliver necessary transport infrastructure for the Games, and devise and implement effective transport plans which provide for legacy use
	Olympic Delivery Authority	2.6	Deliver agreed sustainable legacy plans for the Olympic Park and all venues
	British Olympic Association	2.7	Deliver a viable London Olympic Institute

Strategic objective	Lead stakeholder		Sub-objective
3 To maximise the economic, social, health and environmental benefits of the Games for the UK, particularly through regencration and sustainable development in East London	**Government**	3.1	**Maximise the economic, social, health and environmental benefits the Games bring to the UK and all sections of the UK population**
	Department for Education and Skills and Department for Work and Pensions	3.1.1	Maximise the employment and skills benefits for the UK arising from Games-related business
	Department for Culture, Media and Sport and Department for Trade and Industry	3.1.2	Maximise the wider economic benefits of the Games across the UK, including those for tourism and business promotion
	Department for Culture, Media and Sport	3.1.3	Maximise cultural benefits from hosting the Games and the Cultural Olympiad
	Department of Health, Department for Education and Skills and Cabinet Office	3.1.4	Maximise social benefits, including in health, education and volunteering, of hosting the Games
	Department for Communities and Local Government	3.1.5	Ensure that the Games contribute to Sustainable Communities priorities, including the wider Thames Gateway
	Department for Environment, Food and Rural Affairs	3.1.6	Agree and promote sustainable development and procurement policies, including commitments to sustainable energy and waste management goals
	Foreign and Commonwealth Office	3.1.7	Promote positive images of the UK to an international audience
	Department for Communities and Local Government	3.1.8	Ensure the UK's diverse communities are engaged with, and benefit from, the changes and opportunities arising from hosting the Games in the UK
	Mayor of London	3.2	**Maximise the economic, social, health and environmental benefits the Games bring to London and all Londoners**
	London Development Agency	3.2.1	Maximise the employment and skills benefits for Londoners arising from Games-related business
	London Development Agency	3.2.2	Maximise the wider economic benefits of the Games to London, including those for tourism and business promotion
	Greater London Authority	3.2.3	Maximise cultural benefits to Londoners from hosting the Games and the Cultural Olympiad
	Department of Health, Learning and Skills Council and London Development Agency	3.2.4	Maximise social benefits to Londoners, including in health, education and volunteering, of hosting the Games
	Greater London Authority	3.2.5	Ensure that the Games contribute to Sustainable Communities priorities, including the London Thames Gateway
	Greater London Authority	3.2.6	Agree and promote sustainable development and procurement policies, including commitments to sustainable energy and waste management goals
	Visit London	3.2.7	Promote London's image as a leading world city to an international audience
	Greater London Authority	3.2.8	Ensure London's diverse communities are engaged with, and benefit from, the changes and opportunities arising from hosting the Games in London

Strategic objective	Lead stakeholder		Sub-objective
4 To achieve a sustained improvement in UK sport before, during and after the Games, in both elite performance – particularly in Olympic and Paralympic sports – and grassroots participation	British Olympic Association	4.1	Secure UK Olympic and Paralympic athletes' success in the Games
	Department for Culture, Media and Sport and UK Sport	4.2	Maximise British athlete success in the Olympic and Paralympic Games through investing funds in, and supporting, our most talented athletes
	Department for Culture, Media and Sport and UK Sport	4.3	Secure long term benefits to elite sport competitors – particularly in Olympic and Paralympic sports
	Department for Culture, Media and Sport and Sport England	4.4	Maximise increase in UK participation at community and grassroots level in all sport and across all groups
	Mayor of London	4.5	Maximise increase in London participation at community and grassroots level in all sport and across all groups
	Department for Culture, Media and Sport and Sport England	4.6	Implement viable legacy use for Olympic sports facilities outside London
	Mayor of London	4.7	Implement viable legacy use for Olympic sports facilities in London
	Department for Culture, Media and Sport	4.8	Work with those in other countries, particularly those in development, to promote sport excellence and participation
	British Olympic Association	4.9	Promote, through sport, the Olympic ideals across the 2012 programme

APPENDIX SIX

LOCOG's budget for the London 2012 Olympic and Paralympic Games

1 The London Organising Committee of the Olympic Games and Paralympic Games (LOCOG) is responsible for the operational and staging aspects of the 2012 Games.

2 LOCOG is expected to be self-financing over the course of its existence and has arranged a commercial loan facility of £50 million to fund its activities over the next few years because the majority of its income is not due to be received until 2011 and 2012. LOCOG is expected to receive public funding in 2012 to cover part of the cost of the Paralympics.

3 Any surplus after the Games will be split between the International Olympic Committee (20 per cent), the British Olympic Association (20 per cent), and the general benefit of sport in the UK (60 per cent). In the event of a shortfall between LOCOG's costs and revenues, the Government is the ultimate guarantor.

4 The London 2012 Candidate File included estimates of LOCOG's revenue and expenditure, summarised in the table overleaf. As required by the International Olympic Committee, the estimated budget of £1.5 billion was expressed in 2004 prices. LOCOG has now converted the budget to outturn prices which has produced a cash budget of around £2 billion.

LOCOG's estimated revenue and expenditure, summarised from the London 2012 Candidate File (in 2004 prices)

Revenue	£ million	%	Expenditure	£ million	%
Contribution from the International Olympic Committee for broadcasting rights etc	375	24	Sports venues	261	17
			Information systems	204	13
Ticket sales	310	20	Administration	159	10
Local sponsorship	272	18	Olympic Village and alternative accommodation	136	9
Sponsorship from the Top Olympic Partners programmes	188	12	Transport	124	8
Official suppliers	181	12	Games workforce	117	8
Licensing (merchandise and coin programme)	57	4	Paralympic Games	90	6
Government grant for the Paralympic Games	45	3	Telecommunications and other technologies	63	4
			Advertising and promotion	58	4
Disposal of assets	23	1	Ceremonies and cultural programme	57	3
Other	88	6	International Broadcast Centre and Main Press Centre	29	2
			Security	23	1
			Catering	13	1
			Internet	13	1
			Medical services	12	1
			Pre-Olympic events and co-ordination	12	1
			Other miscellaneous	102	7
			Other contingency	66	4
Total	**1,539**	**100**	**Total**	**1,539**	**100**

Source: London 2012 Candidate File

NOTE

The costs were estimated in pounds sterling but converted into US dollars for the Candidate File, using an exchange rate of £1=$1.6.

Printed in the UK for the Stationery Office Limited
on behalf of the Controller of Her Majesty's Stationery Office
5506260 02/07 65536